INTRODUCTION TO TH

A guide for the novice to the mea
by a leading theorist and

By the same author
THE TAROT OF THE MAGICIANS

INTRODUCTION TO THE STUDY OF THE TAROT

by

Oswald Wirth

Translated from the French by Transcript

THE AQUARIAN PRESS
Wellingborough, Northamptonshire

First published 1981
Second Impression 1983
Third Impression 1984
Fourth Impression 1985

© THE AQUARIAN PRESS 1981

British Library Cataloguing in Publications Data

Wirth, Oswald
    Introduction to the study of the Tarot.
    1. Tarot 2. Cabala
    I. Title II. L'Etude du Tarot. *English*
    133.3'2424   BF1879.T2

    ISBN 0-85030-263-3

Printed and bound in Great Britain

CONTENTS

FOREWORD

The Marquis Stanislas de Guaita (1861–1897) is generally credited with having first introduced the Swiss occultist, Joseph Paul Oswald Wirth (1860–1943), to the magical imagery of the Major Arcana of the tarot pack.

Guaita was himself awakened to occultism by the writings of Alphonse Louis Constant (1810–1875), who wrote under the name Eliphas Lévi. Writing in 1856 in *Rituel de la Haute Magie,* Lévi recognized the need for a complete and well-executed tarot pack, and he expressed the hope that one day he might accomplish the task. Lévi worked for many years on a series of esoteric Major Arcana cards drawn by his own hand and which contained a large number of occult symbols. Lévi was the first person to assign one letter of the Hebrew alphabet to each of the twenty-two Major Arcana cards beginning with Aleph for The Magician, Beth for The Popess, etc. However, Lévi's original tarot designs were never published.

At their first meeting in the spring of 1887, when Guaita learned that Wirth was an amateur artist, the occultist suggested to Wirth that perhaps he might fulfil Lévi's dream of restoring the twenty-two Major Arcana of the tarot to their hieroglyphic purity. Despite no prior knowledge of the tarot, Wirth agreed to accept the charge and under Guaita's guidance he proceeded to design a series of twenty-two Major Arcana cards.

Guaita's knowledge and background of tarot proved especially helpful to Wirth. Despite Guaita's short life span of 36 years, he was in his own right an important figure in French occult circles. In 1888, Guaita founded the Cabalistic Order of the Rosy Cross which counted among its founder members Gerard Encausse (1865–1916) who wrote under the name Papus, Joseph Peladan (1858–1917), and Albert Faucheux (1838–1921) who used the pseudonym Francois-Charles Barlet.

In 1889, Wirth completed the designs for the twenty-two Major Arcana cards and they were issued by E. Poirel in a limited edition of 350 sets under the name, *Les 22 Arcanes du Tarot Kabbalistique*. Each card of Wirth's twenty-two Major Arcana contained an Arabic number from 1 to 21, except the unnumbered card for The Fool. The cards bore a title and each contained the applicable Hebrew letter in accordance with the correspondence assigned by Lévi. Some occult researchers believe the same series of Wirth designs also appeared in 1889 in a book entitled *Le livre de Thot. Les 22 arcanes du Tarot dessines l'usage des inities sur les indications de Stanislas de Guaita*. They were hand coloured and limited to one hundred sets, but this alleged set may be a duplication of information about the series issued by Poirel.

Oswald Wirth's series of the twenty-two Major Arcana cards was one of the earliest occult-orientated, cartomantic packs which realized publication. The designs generally followed the pictorial imagery found in the Tarot of Marseilles deck and the illustrations by Court de Gebelin published in 1787 in 'Du Jeu des Tarot' from *Le Monde Primitif*, but Wirth added numerous alterations to accommodate occult ideas and concepts including those of Lévi and Guaita. For example, two Egyptian sphinxes draw a canopied vehicle in The Chariot (7) card; a serpent appears in front of The Hermit (8); a serpent is entwined around the base of The Wheel of Fortune (10); The Devil (15) depicts a repellent figure with goat's head, bat's wings, cloven feet and the words COAGULA and SOLVE on his arms; and a crocodile appears in The Fool (22) card and the figure of The Fool bears a grotesque face.

Wirth followed the tradition of Lévi and, within the sequence of the Hebrew alphabet, he assigned The Fool card to a position between the Judgement (20) and The World (21) cards with the result its applicable Hebrew letter became *Shin*. However, in the Arabic sequence, The Fool was designated 22 or 0. Thus, the last card of the series also served as the introduction or beginning to the series. The Magician (1) bore the first letter of the Hebrew alphabet, *Aleph*.

The Chariot card in Wirth's deck resembles an illustration of The Chariot card which first appeared in Lévi's *Dogme et Rituel de la Haute Magie,* and which apparently was drawn by Lévi as evidenced by the name 'A. Constant' which appears across the bottom of the card. *Dogme et Rituel de la Haute Magie* was subsequently translated into English by Arthur Edward Waite and is available today under the title *Transcendental Magic*. The Chariot card included by Lévi in his book is not the same design as Lévi's hand-drawn card from his unpublished series of esoteric tarot drawings.

The cards from Wirth's first set of Major Arcana, along with reproductions of traditional Tarot of Marseilles designs, appear in Papus' *Le Tarot des Bohemiens* published in 1889, the same year as the Wirth cards. Five original Wirth cards (9 The Hermit, 13 Death, 14 Temperance, 15 The Devil and 16 The Tower) are reproduced in *The Encyclopedia of Tarot* (1978) by the present writer (Volume I, page 162), and The Devil appears in colour plate number 12.

Wirth also wrote a brief summary of tarot entitled an 'Essay on the Astronomical Tarot' which appeared in Papus' *Le Tarot des Bohemiens.* Wirth espoused the theory of Paul Christian, pseudonym of Jean-Baptiste Pitois, who suggested that the twenty-two Major Arcana cards were originally displayed in two rows of parallel columns in an ancient Egyptian gallery that the neophyte was obliged to enter during initiation. Wirth described the cards as groups or sets of four cards. Thus, cards 2, 3, 4 and 5 formed one group opposite cards 21, 20, 19 and 18. Similarly, cards 7, 8, 9 and 10 combined to form a group opposite 16, 15, 14 and 13. The remaining six Major Arcana contained their own important significance, the two centre cards, 6 and 17, serving as a link between the groups of four cards, and the outer cards on both ends, 1, 11, 12 and 0, forming in themselves a fifth group. In 1896 *Le Tarot des Bohemiens* was translated into English and it is available in occult bookstores as *The Tarot of the Bohemians*.

The foundation of secret occult societies and the idea of initiation of neophytes through the mysterious wisdom of the tarot led to a growing interest in tarot cards and the desire to learn and understand their secrets. One of these societies – The Hermetic Order of the Golden Dawn which was founded in London in 1888 by the Rev. A. F. A. Woodford, Dr. W. R. Woodman and Dr. Wynn Westcott – delved deeply into the tarot.

Arthur Edward Waite, the renowned occultist and prolific writer who was also a member of the Golden Dawn, is known today among tarot devotees as the inspirer of the Rider-Waite tarot deck drawn by Pamela Colman Smith and first published in 1910. Not only does the Rider-Waite deck comprise the full 78 cards consisting of the twenty-two Major Arcana and the fifty-six Minor Arcana, but the latter group, which resembles in structure and numerical value the four suits found in a deck of regular playing cards, also contains a complete scene or picture on each card of the Minor Arcana to assist in the interpretation of the card.

Waite made two important changes from Wirth's Major Arcana cards. Waite switched Justice (8) and Strength (11) to numbers 11 and 8, respectively, and he placed The Fool card at the front of the Major Arcana sequence as number 0 instead of at the end of the sequence. Thus, The Fool, which was assigned the Hebrew letter *Shin* by Wirth, was reassigned by Waite with the letter Aleph, The Magician was assigned Beth, and so on. It is from Wirth's cartomantic designs of the nineteenth century that many tarot packs of the twentieth century take their inspiration, some following the Wirth sequence and others, like Waite, injecting their own modifications. Thus, the importance of Wirth's early efforts and accomplishments cannot be overemphasized.

In 1927, thirty years after Guaita's death, Wirth issued his detailed, encyclopaedic summary of tarot under the title *Le Tarot des imagiers du moyen age*. The book is illustrated with improved designs of

Wirth's earlier twenty-two Major Arcana cards, undertaken with Guaita's approval prior to his death.

The revised version of Wirth's twenty-two Major Arcana cards contains subtle modifications from the original designs. For example, two of the three coins on The Magician's (1) table have been eliminated and the design on the remaining coin has been altered from a six-sided pentacle to a crossed line with four distinct points; The Popess (2) changes slightly the position she faces and the left arm of her throne now depicts a sphinx; the Empress (3) rests her foot on an inverted, instead of upright, quarter moon; The Emperor's (4) knee armour is removed, his upraised staff is more ornate, and the throne upon which he sits is turned so that one side faces the viewer; the figure of winged Cupid in The Lovers (6) card is no longer blindfolded; and the figure of Justice (8) wears a necklace of loosely interwoven chain instead of flat metal links. Additionally, the lion in the Strength (11) card has a tightly curled mane of hair instead of a wavy mane and the claws on his right front paw are extended as they grasp at the ground; the skeleton figure of Death (13) is shown with a smile and the decapitated heads on the ground are larger in size; The Devil (15) appears with a large pentagram on its forehead; the original Tower (16) card with its sixteen falling bricks and sixteen falling wavy droplets is changed to show seven falling bricks and sixteen multi-coloured circles; and The World (21) card depicts a nude, female figure that is less attractive and detailed than the original version. Generally speaking, the revised version of Wirth's cards depicts figures with more attractive facial features and the overall artwork is more artistically executed.

The *Introduction to the Study of the Tarot* by Wirth, first published in Paris in 1931, expounds Wirth's theories of the Major Arcana cards including their initiatory meanings, use and interpretations. Wirth associates the cards in pairs and with this key he proceeds to unfold a story which unlocks the symbolism of the cards. For divination, Wirth recommends a method that employs five cards based upon the inquirer's selection of numbers. Wirth refers to the twenty-two cards as 'Arcana', rather than 'Major Arcana', due to his preoccupation with only the twenty-two Major Arcana, instead of the entire seventy-eight-card deck with its fifty-six Minor Arcana cards which was popularly used for the so-called game of tarot.

Wirth provides key interpretations for each of the twenty-two Major Arcana cards. Yet, he is sufficiently perceptive and sensitive in his viewpoint to admit that symbols do not impose themselves on the mind in the manner of written productions. Rather, they serve to make us think – a catalyst for dreams, inspirations and goals – and, since the capacity of the mind is infinite, so too is there no end to the suggestive power of the tarot. Therein lies the compelling force of tarot cards that fascinates, challenges and stimulates each of us to greater heights and, perhaps, to fuller lives.

The revised set of Wirth's twenty-two Major Arcana cards was reprinted in 1966 in France and a full pack of seventy-eight cards comprising the twenty-two Major Arcana and fifty-six Minor Arcana cards is available today as the Oswald Wirth Tarot deck. Readers in the United Kingdom interested in the complete Oswald Wirth Tarot deck should contact Aquarian Press. In the United States, the Oswald Wirth Tarot deck is available from U. S. Games Systems, Inc., New York, New York 10016 and Samuel Weiser, Inc., York Beach, Maine 03910.

Stuart R. Kaplan,
New York, 1981.

1

THE DECIPHERMENT OF THE
TWENTY-TWO ARCANA

Would you like to understand imagery without being limited to the way of reading, based on the alphabet, that is taught to children? Have you heard of a *universal book,* open to all but not written in ordinary letters?

There is such a book, and it gives a comprehensive view of those things which show themselves to our senses and our imagination. This book is dumb: it is nothing but a collection of fascinating pictures. As we turn its pages we admire the shapes and colours, but without guessing the meaning of the motley parade we find so diverting. We have so little time to spare from our everyday affairs that we have none to give to meditation any more. For information we turn to textbooks and encyclopaedias, certain that we shall find the answers to our questions in them.

But by doing this we are losing the habit of making independent discoveries by engaging in deep thought. We are constantly absorbing other men's notions and our intellectual life is not our own. A moment's pause will bring the realization of how humiliating this is. Is there nothing in our mental sphere we can really call our own? Our wealth of ideas is rarely self-created, when all is said and done, and does not compare with the thoughts of some illiterate person who has given himself to reflection and has acquired a fund of original ideas born of his own, unaided mental activity.

There are certain people who pride themselves on being 'free-thinkers', and set themselves up in opposition to traditional beliefs. Whatever is affirmed by the orthodox believers they systematically deny, believing that this puts them in possession of incontrovertible truth. These self-appointed thinkers have not even begun to learn to think, and in fact the very last thing they can do is to think freely, for they are content to revert to verbal formulae put into circulation like paper money but without any intrinsic value.

What I am pleading for is that people should stop confusing living pure thought with its expression through the medium of *words*. Speech is always misleading because it is incapable of conveying everything that is in the mind, hence the fatal folly of human arguments.

The wisdom of the ancients assures us that 'the naked Truth lies hid at the bottom of a well.' * This *naked* Truth is that which is not disguised by any expression. The only place where we can find it is in ourselves, within the dark depths of our personalities; but it is not within the power of *words* to evoke it. A word summons up an idea that has already been formulated, one of the vagrant phantoms of the Astral Light of the occultists. Passive clairvoyants attract such formations in order to embody them in their imaginations. Therefore what they reveal can bear on objects of great interest, but with no guarantee of accuracy.

The mind perceives things in a different way when it is put in the presence of objective images, on which it exercises its wit in order to discern what they signify. This time other faculties come into play. *Active divination* is not content to offer the mirror of imagination to anything which chooses to be reflected in it; it meditates, reflects intensely, searches, reasons, compares, until an Apollonian light rises in the spirit.

But what is meant by this *active divination*? It is here that the study of the Tarot recommends itself, not, at least at the start, by reading the

---

* *Oswald Wirth has combined two old proverbs here.* [Translator's note]

interpretative works published on the subject. All that should be done is simply to procure the twenty-two Arcana (i.e. the Tarot trump cards), restored as faithfully as possible in accordance with the spirit of their symbolism.[1]

These images have been combined in such a way as to lead a discerning mind to discover for itself what they signify. Hence there should be nothing arbitrary about the interpretation of the Tarot, called that 'marvel of the human spirit' by the brilliant occultist Eliphas Lévi, whose enthusiasm is fully justified. We have confirmed his opinion that nothing has been left to chance in the composition of the true Tarot, reduced to the twenty-two philosophical keys (which comprise a set that is quite distinct from the game of cards with which it is associated).*

[1] We applied ourselves to this task in preparing the eleven illuminated plates accompanying the *Tarot of the Mediaeval Picture Makers*. Our advice is not to read the book until work has been done on the pictures, studying them abstractly apart from any preconceived theory.

* Wirth is perhaps a little too dismissive here. Papus and others have certainly attached great importance to this so-called 'game of cards' or the 'Minor Arcana' as some prefer to name them. Contemplation of their designs as preserved in the best packs can be quite instructive. [*Translator's note.*]

There are twenty-two pictures. Why so? This number is that of the letters in the primitive alphabet. Is this a coincidence? All the pictures are numbered except one, which therefore corresponds to zero. The numbered cards form a group of 21, a number with the traditionally sacred numbers 3 and 7 as its factors.

Before contemplating each image in isolation, it is as well to take a look at the laws underlying the construction of the Tarot as a whole. How do the twenty-two Arcana fit together? They follow one another in numerical order from 1 to 21, with zero at the end or, looked at another way, at the beginning in front of the 1. The two positions for zero are reconciled by disposing the cards in the form of a wheel as suggested by the name Rota, a variant on the word Tarot.

The circular arrangement leads us to distinguish, as in the terrestrial globe, two opposite hemispheres, or to put it more simply, a northern row and a southern row. For ease of comparison, these semicircular rows are aligned along their common equator, and it then appears that they are polarized inversely; for, at first sight, the ordered images in the north row follow one another in a direction opposite to that followed by the corresponding images in the south row.

Therefore, the Tarot is double: masculine-active from 1 to 11 and feminine-passive from 12 to 0.

This is not all. A group of four is formed by Arcana 2, 3, 4 and 5, showing the Empress and Emperor flanked by the Popess and the Pope (pp. 18, 19).

These four cards constitute a distinct set, the significance of which requires study. And since there is already a correspondence, by the analogy of contraries, between one Tarot row and the other, it may reasonably be expected that Arcana 18, 19, 20 and 21 will comprise a similar set (pp. 20, 21).

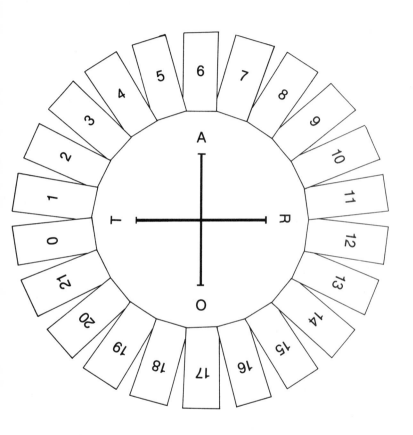

le Jugement

le Monde

Considerations of symmetry then indicate that there will be two other sets of four composed of Arcana 7, 8, 9, 10 (p. 23) and 13, 14, 15, 16 (p. 24).

Thus, we have four sets headed (on the outside) by Arcana 1, 11, 12 and 0. These make up a fifth set of four when taken by themselves (p. 25).

Nevertheless, it is preferable to retain the last-mentioned cards in the positions they occupy in the Tarot in relation to one another, for they do not follow each other in numerical order but constitute what we will term a *tetrad*. By this we mean a double relationship, involving at one and the same time lateral analogies (between 1 and 0, 1 and 11, 11 and 12, 12 and 0) and diametrical oppositions (between 1 and 12, 11 and 0). A glance at the diagram will make this plain.

And so we are left with two independent cards in the centres of the two rows: 6 and 17 (pp. 26, 27) ; as if they were neutral or perhaps forming a link between the Arcana ranged on either side of them.

le Bateleur

la Force

le Fou

le Pendu

It is worthwhile paying some attention to this constructional plan of the Tarot if we wish to learn what the twenty-two Arcana have to say to us, because it supplies an interpretative key of capital importance. In fact, the Arcana are divided into four regions which may be designated by the points of the compass; with the north row divided into north-west and north-east and the south row divided into south-east and south-west. But if north and south signify male activity and female passivity, what is the meaning of east and west?

It will be seen that from 1 to 11, the Arcana go from east to west and, from 12 to 0 they go from west to east. Now this is how the candidate for initiation perambulates his Lodge when taking his obligations.

Light comes from the East, where it is renewed each morning. The candidate turns towards this source of illumination because he flees the darkness which invades the West where the Sun sets. It seems likely that the person of the candidate is recognizable in the *Juggler* with his paraphernalia. If so, then the *Popess, Empress, Emperor* and *Pope* represent those who successively initiate and instruct him.

Arcanum 6 has obviously been inspired by mythology, being none other than young Hercules choosing his path at the end of his apprenticeship. Although tempted by Indolence to enjoy the pleasures of life, he heeds the voice of Virtue, who urges him to perform great and noble deeds.

It must be admitted that the Tarot's Entered Apprentice chose the good path, for Arcana 7, 8, 9, 10 and 11 lead him on to the most enviable achievements. Knowing how to rule himself, he drives his *Chariot* in triumph. Having become a balanced person, he adopts a coordinating role and, like *Justice*, brings equity into every situation. What is more, he lives the life of a sage detached from human vanities, like a *Hermit* inaccessible to the frivolous world. And so, desiring nothing, he dominates the *Wheel of Fortune*, indifferent to the ups and downs of Fate. Finally, he possesses that intellectual and moral *Strength* which overcomes violence, and exercises a calm which tames all fierceness. This is the ideal character of the peacemaker, of the Initiate with spiritual power, of the Craftsman who knows how to work on the Cubic Stone.

The Master has to make progress by retracing his steps. Moving from 12 to 13, he will go to 0 and regain his point of departure subterraneously. In self-renunciation he will experience the powerlessness of the *Hanged Man*, after vanquishing the supreme human force (11). He will learn complete detachment in order to pass through, in experience, the gates of *Death*. Untroubled by the fear of dying, he will find Life, ever flowing from one vessel to the other in the hands of *Temperance*. The Master, who has been cleansed of all defilement by the laving tide, then approaches the *Devil*, the great regenerator of universal driving force. It is necessary for him to come to terms with the Prince of this World in order to compel him to achieve the Great Work, for the demons of materiality, whom the adept must know how to exorcise, have made themselves at home in terrestrial conditions more readily than have the angels flying in the ethereal spheres. But the task is toilsome, the Art is difficult and checks are inevitable; we must be aware of the catastrophe of the *Falling Tower*. Must we allow ourselves to be paralysed by the threat of the collapse of our dream? No! Let us be bold! The heavens can not awe the Titan who does not tremble at the lightning.* What does it matter if we fall when Hope can raise us up again? In our night, the *Stars* are shining and the ideal is our guide. We must strive to learn to discern illusion on entering the path of hard work. Everything deceives us and we fall from one deception into another, but we go on, fascinated by the *Moon*. While still chasing moonbeams, we come to the end of our road and, when the pale disc sets the *Sun* rises. He brings us at last the True Light, which enlightens our minds and rescues Humanity from the errors under which it is labouring. Then comes the *Judgement*: the dead are resurrected and the Initiates rediscover the Lost Word. Hiram rises, the Past lives again in whatever it held of the precious and imperishable for the future. Now order is brought out of chaos, the Temple is built and the *World* appears as a harmonious Whole. But the last word of Wisdom belongs to the Fool, who leads us to the knowledge of the Nothingness† from which everything has come forth.

The object of the above sketch is to throw a ray of light on the initiatory meaning of the twenty-two Tarot cards. We have posed a

* The original text says, 'The Heavens are not too high for the Titan who ...', but this seems to fly in the face of the whole lesson conveyed by the Greek myth [*Translator's note.*]

† *Ain*, or the Negative Existence of the Qabalah. [*Translator's note.*]

problem without solving it here. The solutions are to be found in my book on the *Tarot of the Mediaeval Picture-Makers*, which cost me forty years of research and meditation to prepare.

I would urge the serious student not to be in too much of a hurry to read my text; this would be shirking the desirable effort to fathom the meaning of the cards for himself. It is preferable to follow my own example and examine the twenty-two Arcana taken from a good Tarot pack. My reconstitution, in eleven plates, of this masterpiece of the Picture-Makers of the Middle Ages is especially suitable for such strictly personal study. Later on, it will be interesting to compare findings, but the person who makes no attempt to work things out for himself makes no more progress than the schoolboy using a crib – that is to say he makes none at all. Enthusiasts have the advantage of making a direct attack on the enigma. I need do hardly more than give them one or two hints.

It is useless to start by worrying about the range of interpretations connected with each card. Meritorious and fruitful work consists in discovering for oneself these interpretations, which have not been settled once for all. Symbols do not impose themselves on the mind in the manner of written productions: they make us think and, since the field of thought is infinite, there is no end to what they suggest. We praise *symbolism* because we see in it a most powerful stimlator of independent thought drawing strength from within itself. Philosophers who squabble over words deafen us with their jabber and far from helping us to think freely they attempt to convert us to their pet systems. Now symbols are superior because, being dumb, they preach nothing but appeal entirely to reflection. Respecting the liberty, even of lazy brains, they keep themselves from tyranny, for those who despise symbols are not detained by them. But those who are led to meditation by symbols stay with them, for an image keeps the mind tirelessly at work. The first spontaneous idea leads to another, which provokes a third, and so on in an uninterrupted chain. Nothing can stop the thinker who knows how to think for himself, inspired by what is suggested to him by the sight of things. Before there are any words, thought comes naturally to the one who is reflecting contemplatively. It is then translated into a dreamlike vision which illuminates the mind. The seer perceives in his own way but remains dumb, unable to find the words which would enable him to speak. Nevertheless, what he has conceived torments him; he feels the need to communicate his dream and forces himself to recount his vision. Thus is born the poet, the chanter of songs, the rhapsodist. He speaks in an imagery that evokes dreams, and so his vision tends to communicate itself to contemplatives familiar with silent reverie.

All this being so, need we be surprised at the law of silence that has always been imposed on Initiates? To *be silent* is their first rule. It is not so much that they fear indiscrete revelations, for the secret of thought is safe from being divulged, but the master has to maintain silence in order to constrain the disciple to reflect, and the disciple must submit to the discipline of silence so that he may profit by a form of instruction that each of us can derive from himself.

So here we are in the presence of the Tarot, a book that is intentionally mute, an exceptional initiatory document of the first rank. We should learn to appreciate this masterpiece of the Middle Ages; worthy of our admiration to the same extent as are the Gothic cathedrals and philosophic Alchemy. Unknown sages have bequeathed to us the treasure of their mysterious knowledge. Their message is, '*We inculcate nothing, we provoke reflection*', and they invite us *to initiate ourselves*. But to what? To the magical secrets of the thaumaturgists of all ages? Yes, but incidentally, in consequence of the development of a divinatory power unlimited in its applications. We are dealing here with revelations much more serious than those of all the occultisms. What is in question is the *Art of thought*, which is the supreme Art, the *Great Art*, rightly known as the *Royal Art*, because it is designed to make *Kings*.

The *Realm* that has to be conquered is that of the *Spirit*. In Hebrew it is called *Malkuth* and seems not to be of this world. Certainly not, if by 'world' we understand the domain of everyday competition and of gross objectivity. The effective Thinker is in touch with a *World* to which allusion is made in the twenty-first Arcanum of the Tarot. Although it does not come within the range of our material senses, this world is *real*, with a reality better guaranteed than that of the phantasmagoria of physical appearances.

It is important to work and take pains, to be purposeful, when one enters the field of the Tarot. Work is essential, for without work it will give you nothing! I have laboured long in this field and I have taken from it a treasure which has brought me so much richness of the imagination that I would not sell it for a million pounds. Since it is spiritual, the treasure belonging to the thinker is inexhaustible; no use can deplete it. There is no comparison between it and dead material treasure. On the contrary, it is a living spring, the flow from which responds to our needs. It is the Infinite that pours forth the Water that slakes the Spirit's thirst.

These are merely images, and everything is no more than a show of images in the last analysis. However, we must learn to comprehend images if we would decipher those of the Tarot.

2

WHAT THE CARDS SAY

Knowing the plan of construction of the Tarot, we possess the key to its symbolism; however, some help is needed in using this key. The main secret is to put the characters together in pairs and to listen to their conversation, as it were.

First, confront the *Juggler* and the *Fool* and see how they react to one another.

Because he heads the twenty-two Arcana, the Juggler is conscious of being the great Beginner and recognizes in the Fool the ultimate Ender. All things begin with *One* and end in *Nought*. This initial discovery could have a big effect on the mind which is in sympathy with the Juggler. Such a mind will tend to be restless and to make itself dizzy by spinning a thousand theories, each succeeding one being more seductive than the last. It devotes itself to learning and dazzles itself and others.

Opposed to the Juggler, the agile illusionist, is the unreflecting Fool, indifferent to his fate and a creature of impulse. The Fool responds passively to events and is free from ambitions and cares.

We might do well to meditate on these personages and ask ourselves if there is not something of each of them in us.

Initiatory wisdom helps us to avoid being deceived by the Juggler without abandoning ourselves to the impulsiveness of the Fool. *In medio stat virtus* (virtue is in the middle). While seeking a sensible happy medium, we ought not entirely to repudiate the 'Folly' of which Erasmus wrote 'in praise'. We must know how to be foolish to the extent of gaining true wisdom.

Since, as we have seen, 11 is the outcome of 1 in the active series, just as 12 leads to 0 in the passive series, it seems good to refer to cards 11 (*Strength*) and 12 (the *Hanged Man*) when seeking to explain numbers 1 (the *Juggler*) and O (the *Fool*).

In the end the cleverness of the Juggler is his Strength. Intelligence imposes its discernment on brutality. The passionate lion is tamed and serene wisdom is victorious, man's knowledge triumphs and reason reigns.

But then everything is going well. We stay as we are, not wishing to proceed further; there seems no point in going on to 12 which would lead us to O.

Let us be on our guard against the Juggler and his promises. Pure reason shines in philosophy in the realm of abstractions, but in practical life it is liable to prove fallacious.

Let us heed the *Hanged Man*, who has not shrunk from self-renunciation. Unlike the Juggler, he has no confidence in his own power or in the energy that is in him, but he places himself at the disposal of a will that is greater than his. His dream is to obey One whose decisions are higher than his own. There he is, voluntarily reduced to personal impotence. His arms have been tied behind his back and, instead of standing upright in the normal way on the ground of practical reality, he is suspended by one foot from the dead wood of mystical power.

This tortured prisoner, who is seen to be smiling, is diametrically opposed to the Juggler, just as Strength is opposed to the Fool. By placing the four cards in front of us we can stimulate the flowering of our thoughts, and the wise man will undertake to marry within himself Strength and the Hanged Man.

le Bateleur

la Force

le Fou

le Pendu

Once the set of four cards just considered has ceased speaking, others can be set side by side to speak in their turn. It will be enough to set them out, for the reader is not deaf; he will understand these silent characters when they are able to awake in him an echo of unuttered truths.

Here are four aspects of the *unknown*.

The mysterious and impenetrable *Popess* (2) has to do with whatever remains hidden though vaguely sensed by our intuition. The high priestess of the Mysteries is the first to instruct us because we owe to her our premonitions and every idea that presents itself spontaneously in the mind.

In passive opposition to her is the *World* (21), the synthesis of everything which falls within the scope of our senses. This is an enigmatic manifestation, for nothing is more unknown to us than that which is translated for us into sensations (p. 37).

Hence it is our duty to decipher the hieroglyphics of objectivity by means of our divinatory faculties. If we allow ourselves to be duped by appearances we shall never succeed in lifting the veil hanging between the two columns of the Binary at the entrance to the sanctuary of Knowledge (Gnosis).

The *Wheel of Fortune* (10) carries us into the unknown areas of daily life. We live without knowing what that life is in the vortex of which we are caught. It drags us round from high to low and so on as if all depended on the whims of chance.

The vital circuit is interrupted by *Death* (13), which has no power to destroy, however, for everything is transformed and incessantly dies to be reborn (p. 38).

The man in the street does not know the great secret of renewal; he is absorbed in his temporary life (Arc. 10) and does not know how to comply with the law of permanent life, which lays down that we must keep dying in order to live regenerated.

Now let us move on from the set of four cards representing what is impenetrable to the set representing what is *intelligible* (p. 39).

Mother of those ideas which make up the subtle plane of things, the *Empress* (3) is lifted above the level of action. She is that Wisdom which conceives the executive act; she reigns as the supreme inspirer of whatever is consciously accomplished.

The analogy of contraries sets her beside the *Judgement* (20), the final appraisal of accomplished facts. The latter may not all have been premeditated, but their spontaneity is never blind. Acting without knowing why, we can respond to an unconscious inspiration from which pure hearts may benefit, inspired by a righteous piety.

Therefore, we should employ our intelligence as much as possible to understand matters (Arc. 3) but should also pay attention to our noble feelings when they incite us to kind deeds.

The wisdom of the heavenly *Virgin* (Arc. 3) communicates itself to the wise *Hermit* (9), who withdraws himself to avoid distractions. He goes on his earthly way with prudence, probing the ground before him with his staff and illuminating it with the flickering light from his lantern.

The passive counterpart to this philosophy deprived of wings is the winged angel of *Temperance* (14), dispenser of the vital fluid. Temperance seems to say, 'Do not isolate yourself – bathe in the tide of life. Purify yourself and fear nothing!'

Here again, we learn to keep between the two columns; so that we can shut ourselves away deliberately on some occasions and judiciously come out into the open on others. We can ripen our own fruit within us (Arc. 9) yet gather the good things that lie outside us (Arc. 14).

From ideas we pass to *actions*.

The *Emperor* (4) brings into realization what the Empress (3) conceives. What is incarnate in him is active power, represented by the inner Fire, the Sulphur of the Alchemists

The infernal fire, without which no work could be carried out, is not essentially different from that which flames in the *Sun* (19), but the plutonian heat labours obscurely, whereas the celestial brightness floods out triumphantly.

Illuminating the mind, it brings peace and harmony to mankind; nevertheless, earthly paradise (Arc. 19) can be regained only by the

persistent labour of Vulcan (Arc. 4). It is essential to will with energy
(Arc. 4) in order to conquer the redemptive Light (Arc. 19).

What the Emperor (4) achieves is *Justice* (8). This introduces order into whatever is confused and ceaselessly organizes chaos, bringing about law and order by the workings of equilibrium. All things are balanced in the incessant movement of life.

Yet everything is not uniform in this vital rhythm with its alternate accelerations and decelerations. Consequently there are difficulties every now and then available to be exploited by the *Devil* (15), drawn here as a caricature of the classical god Pan, the universal guide of the animal instincts.

If equilibrium (Arc. 8) were never disturbed life would flow smoothly without producing anything special or extraordinary. Crises release energy fueling the effort which overcomes the difficulties involved. It is good to have the 'devil in the body' in order to bring into play the latent resources in our productive powers.

The final set of four cards is concerned with religion under its conflicting aspects.

Religion is born of the control we exercise over our 'good' or 'evil' actions. The individual who believes in social decencies submits himself to a system of ethis such as might be formulated by our Tarot *Pope* (5). This conscious and active type of religion proceeds from the internal arbiter who regulates our impulses.

If we uncritically abandon ourselves to religious sentimentality, we shall fall into superstition, which is ruled by the Moon (18), the (astrological) planet of the imagination.

Self-mastery as taught by the Pope (5) makes a person worthy to occupy the *Chariot* (7) drawn by two sphinxes, one black and the other white, the respective symbols of selfish instincts and generous impulses. The charioteer keeps the vehicle moving along the middle track. He avoids all deviations and has in view an ideal earthly religion: that of the wise conduct of life.

Opposing this judicious practice of the art of living are the ambitions of the *Falling Tower* also known as the *House of God* (16). The mystic wishes to build a tower reaching to the heavens while the vulgar mind materializes holy things. Between them both a catastrophe is inevitable.

Nevertheless, room must be given both for the flights of mysticism and for the needs of materiality which give rise to the various forms of worship (Arc. 16). Superstitions (Arc. 18) must not be censured too severely provided morals (Arc. 5) render them innocuous and the cultivation of religious sentiment is translated into an exemplary accomplishment of the duties of life (Arc. 7).

Two of the Tarot trumps do not enter into any of the sets of four we have been considering. These constitute the axis of the Tarot, and divide it vertically as if to separate theory from practice, the acquisition of knowledge from its application.

The *Lovers* (6) is significant in this respect, because the young man (like the youthful Hercules) is choosing between two paths, that of heroism and that of indulgence. His education is over and he has to decide how to employ the talents he has developed.

The *Star* (17) refrains from decision-making, like the passive subject who accepts his destiny as the docile instrument of the power that leads him through the starry night of his life.

It is certain that not everything depends on our free will. Naturally, we should use our brains to avoid faults and to direct ourselves more effectively towards some recognized goal (Arc. 6); but we must learn to accept decisions taken on our behalf by life without consulting us. Let us have faith in our star (17), which guides us without telling us where we are going.

The time has now come to recapitulate by going over very quickly what has been said about the twenty-two Arcana.

Taking advantage of the fact that he possesses all capabilities, the *Juggler* (1) enters in turn the schools of the *Popess* (2), the *Empress* (3), the *Emperor* (4) and the *Pope* (5), learning successively to distrust the unknowable (Arc. 2), to conceive clear ideas (Arc. 3), to exercise his will (Arc. 4) and to rely on his own actions (Arc. 5). When his Apprenticeship is over, he becomes a Fellow Craftsman like the youth in the *Lovers* (6) and proves that he knows how to drive the *Chariot* (7). Then he administers with *Justice* (8) the goods with which he has been entrusted, while preserving a disinterested attitude like the *Hermit* (9) in his appreciation of riches. In this way he will dominate the *Wheel of Fortune* (10) and will deploy his *Strength* (11).

Strong in knowledge and firm of will, the positive Initiate has the option of confining himself to rational accomplishments without aspiring to go beyond his rôle of skilled Craftsman. Having travelled along the way of *purgation* and the way of *illumination*, he is not obliged to enter the way of *union*, which is that of the higher mystic and of the fully initiated Master. Here all proceeds from a sacrifice, implying total self-renunciation and the acceptance of the torture endured by the smiling *Hanged Man* (12). Repudiating all egoism, the subject of the Great Work dies in the Middle Chamber; but *Death* (13) prepares him for complete vivifying transmutation. The waters of *Temperance* (14) are those of universal Life. The individual who bathes in them no longer lives strictly for himself. Thus, baptized in Jordan, he can venture into the wilderness and confront the *Devil* (15), the eternal tempter of the passions, who obeys when he can not command because resistance to his temptations reduces him to slavery. But here is the *Falling Tower* (16), that presumptious building of equivocal certitudes which will be avoided by the Initiate, for he does not fear to live without shelter under the protection of the *Star* (17), the sparkling lights of our dreams and of free mystical illumination. However, the independent truth-seeker has to face the path of misery winding over that treacherous ground which is lit so deceptively by the *Moon* (18). In spite of all false steps and falls, if the journey continues until dawn, the Sun (19) will rise at last as the shedder of *true light*! When this triumphs, the *Judgement* (20), which revives the past, will sound its arrival. Hiram rejuvenated will rise from his grave. After this, with the Temple completed, the *World* (21) will be harmoniously built. And yet, all around will be the domain of the Fool (0), the bottomless pit personified by the primordial Babylonian god Abzu.

One can not help wondering whether this rapid review will really be enough to give some idea of the value of the Tarot. However, for the individual who intends to reflect on his own in order to work out an independent philosophy, not drawn from books but from the symbolical well where Truth lies hid, no exercise will be more beneficial than persevering meditation based on a discerning comparison of the twenty-two pictures bequeathed to us by the Middle Ages.

3

PRACTISING DIVINATION

In disdaining the imagination, our rational civilization shows itself inferior to the savage in subtlety. Methodical observations, experiment and calculation have led us to such results that we silence our imaginations when they try to suggest anything to us. This is being far too careful because intuition has such an important part to play in life that it is absurd to try and turn it into an abstraction. Rather than suppressing them fearfully it would surely make more sense to develop our imaginative faculties under the control of reason.

While supporting progress, we should beware falling into the trap of an obscurantism which forbids lucid dreaming, presentiments and divination. We should consider training ourselves to *use our imaginations properly* by methods similar to those which inculcate *correct reasoning*. Certainly, no divination is infallible, but then even the most careful reasoner is liable to be guilty of sophistry at times.

In so far as the imagination is restricted to wandering aimlessly among the images which present themselves to it, its function remains passive or *lunar*. Our incoherent dreams are like this, they are automatic and not suggested by some hidden reality. However, there is no bar to certain spontaneous impressions being revelatory, as proved by premonitions which have turned out to be true and by the facts of telepathy as confirmed by science. But impressionability scarcely lends itself to systematic education; one can not cultivate a natural gift that manifests itself under external influences independent of our free will. Therefore educability is limited to active or *solar* divination and it is that alone we shall be considering here.

The Tarot is the ideal instrument of active divination because it puts the understanding to work. When set in the presence of mute pictures, the human mind interrogates them in order to get (not them but) itself to reply. Solar divination is really a conversation with the part in us that does the thinking. Symbolic pictures stimulate reflection in us just as the objective universe stimulated reflection in the first thinkers of our race. They looked into a book that was there before any written records existed, namely into that immense collection of silent images displayed to us by Nature. The Tarot is similar in character to this book of books and incites us to fathom its meaning as does everything which offers itself to our admiring contemplation.

The Universe speaks to poets, those sons of Apollo, who are sensitive to the beautiful and the sublime, and we too must recognize that however prosaic our world appears to us, it is not exclusively governed by cold prose. Symbolism is inherent in it, and significant images presented to us by the theatre of life. However, we are not claiming that everybody has sufficient insight to read them properly.

Yet they are generally accessible to active imaginations capable of musing without going to extremes. But of course, to use the Tarot as it should be used, it is necessary to master this instrument of divination. Until our minds have entered into rapport with the images that are expected to speak to them, there is a barrier to understanding. Study, such as we would undertake if we had to converse with the speaker of a foreign language, is imperative. We need to familiarize ourselves with the mode of expression of the symbols, as in the exercises recommended in the last two chapters.

Once we have succeeded in our attempts at divination applied to the Tarot, it will become possible for us to extend our range. Everything takes place in the field of the imagination, where one image evokes another. In the alert mind the images summon one another according to the laws of some mysterious affinity. Suggestions arise which answer the purposes of some hidden reality, and the latter intervenes as the deciding factor that brings about the selection of a given interpretation from the many of which a symbol is susceptible.

Incidentally, it is much harder to justify the mechanism of divination than to put it into practice. Just as we can live without a knowledge of physiology and reason in ignorance of the canons of logic, so we can divine without being able to explain how divination works. Nevertheless, certain practical rules must be observed by the diviner who does not wish to stoop to trifling with the curiosity of those who consult him.

First and foremost, it is necessary to be sincere and to hold in horror any kind of deception. Lying is odious in a fortune-teller. Genuine divination is a service performed in the temple of Truth.

Probity and reliability demand that we do not claim the ability to pick up every vibration, and quack promises are unworthy of the serious diviner, who should keep his statements within reasonable bounds. In principle, foretelling the future lies outside the province of active divination; we do not say it is impossible – nor is hitting the bull's-eye with a bullet from a loosely held gun – but a diviner will prefer not to make pronouncements in this respect if he has any scruples. What is said is best confined to the present. The client may have an immediate decision to take or may be on the point of making some mistake; the Tarot can then help him to sort out his impressions and to find the road to a satisfactory solution. The one who reads the cards must not make his oracle too precise or narrow; in doing so he might easily go astray, because there is so much elasticity in the interpretation of the symbols. Often this elasticity will prove to be beneficial, since the sensible client will accept what is said with caution and will wait until the import of the reading suddenly becomes clear to him.* Besides, it is a recognized fact that clients are divided into good

* Sometimes this sudden realization comes too late, as it did with King Crœsus, whose fascinating story is told in Book I of the *Histories* of Herodotus. When he complained of being deceived by the oracle at Delphi, he was told, 'Crœsus has no right to complain; for Apollo foretold him that if he made war on the Persians he would subvert a great empire; and had he desired to be truly informed, he ought to have sent again to inquire, whether his own or that of Cyrus was meant.' Again, speaking of Apollo, who was supposed to inspire the oracle, the Pythian priestess confessed, 'The god himself even can not avoid the decrees of fate'. (Cary's translation). [*Translator's note.*]

and bad; the divination comes out clearly for the good, but the bad seem to inhibit clairvoyance. Some diviners divine the nature of those clients who would prove awkward and refuse to work for them.

Say, for example, it is proposed that the Tarot be consulted on some question judged acceptable; the following procedure is recommended.

The client will start by handing over an offering, which nowadays will at least be a piece of silver money. It is desirable for the diviner not to profit by this payment, because only if he is disinterested in his clairvoyance ensured. However, if he is obliged to live by his art, he should at least give to the poor whatever share of his earnings he can afford. The amateur diviner will keep nothing for himself and will be completely independent in his divination. He will be free from all considerations of keeping and satisfying his clients and will say what he sees without troubling his head about profane contingencies.

Filled with a fervent desire to be useful to the consulter, the diviner shuffles the usual cards numbered from 1 to 22 and then asks his client to tell him the first number between 1 and 22 inclusive that has entered his mind.

The number mentioned is used to cut the pack shuffled by the diviner; starting from the top, it indicates the card that has to be turned up in the pile. This card bears a number which must be noted before it is put back and reshuffled with the others. Exactly the same procedure is followed a second, third and fourth time. On each occasion the number of the card to which the cut is made is counted.

Finally, the four numbers which have been found supply a fifth by addition. This must be reduced theosophically if it is greater than 22 $(23 = 2 + 3 = 5, 47 = 4 + 7 = 11, \text{etc.})$.

Our five numbers designate the Tarot Arcana which make up the oracle when arranged in a cross as follows, in the order in which they were chosen:

Arcana
corresponding to the
third number chosen.

JUDGE
The deciding factor for
or against.

Arcana
corresponding to the first
number chosen

FOR
What is favourable.
What should be done.

Arcana
corresponding to the
number obtained by the
addition of the other four
numbers.

SYNTHESIS
The point at issue. What
matters taking
everything as a whole.

Arcana
corresponding to the
second number chosen

AGAINST
What is unfavourable.
What should be avoided.

Arcana
corresponding to the
fourth number chosen.

SENTENCE
Solution.
Result.

The Arcana laid out opposite one another in this way are mutually explanatory. Whatever the case, the first number selected must receive a favourable interpretation whatever its card, even if unattractive ones like the Hanged Man (12), Death (13), the Falling Tower (16), the Moon (18) or the Fool (22)* are turned up. On the other hand, the second number selected imparts an ill-omened sense to its Arcana, even when the latter is the Chariot (7), Strength (11), the Sun (19) or the World (21).

In order to give some idea of the opposite significations belonging to each Arcana according to whether it has to be taken as lucky or unlucky, we shall end the present brief account with a comparative Table which will assist beginners in finding their bearings in the complexities of the symbolic suggestions.

le fou   ZU

---

* The Fool is not numbered and is thus equivalent to zero; however in divination it counts as 22 according to its place in the pack.

4

THE ARCANA INTERPRETED AS GOOD OR BAD

I **THE JUGGLER. Point of departure, first cause, Mercurial influence**

Dexterity, ability, diplomatic skill, eloquence, the art of persuasion, quick wit, keen intelligence, active business man.

Persuasive braggart, suggestionist, illusionist, schemer, unscrupulous careerist, demagogue, charlatan, impostor, liar, crook, confidence trickster. Much ado about nothing, absence of scruples.

II **THE POPESS. Mystery, intuition, piety, passive Saturnian influence.**

Reserve, discretion, silence, meditation, faith, hope, patience, religious sentiment, resignation, favourable secrets. Necessary inertia.

Hidden intentions, dissimulation, hypocrisy, false assumption that help will be forthcoming, inactivity, laziness. Bigotry, grudges, hostile or apathetic moods, mystical absorption.

III **THE   EMPRESS.   Wisdom,   discernment,   ideality, intellectual solar influence.**

Comprehension, intelligence, instruction, charm, affability, elegance, distinction, courtesy. Mental domination, abundance, riches. Civilization.

Affectation, pose, coquetry, vanity, pretention, disdain, frivolity, ostentation, prodigality. Susceptibility to flattery, lack of refinement, manners of the nouveau-riche.

IV **THE   EMPEROR.   Strength   of   mind,   materialism, executive power, Saturno-Martian influence.**

Privilege, strictness, certitude, fixity, achievement, energy, perserverance, resolute will, carrying out of resolutions. Powerful protector.

Tenacious opposition, mulishness, hostile prejudices, implacable enmity, thwarted enterprise, antagonistic government, great risk of defeat or failure. Tyranny, absolutism.

V **THE   POPE.   Duty,   morality,   conscience,   Jupiterian influence.**

Moral authority, social ministry, observation of the conventions, respectability, teaching, balanced advice, benevolence, generosity, magnanimity, forgiveness, indulgence.

Sententious pundit, rigid moralist, dogmatic metaphysician, dictatorial school teacher, narrow-minded theoretician, pompous preacher. Adviser void of practical common sense.

VI **THE LOVERS. Sensibility, free will, testing. The double influence of Venus or to speak more carefully of Ishtar, warlike as the morning star and amorous as the evening star.**

Willed determinism, choice, vows, aspirations, desires. Examination, deliberations, responsibility. Affections, sympathies.	Trials, doubt, irresolution. Dangerous temptations, risk of seduction, loose living, licentious ways, feebleness, lack of heroism.

VII **THE CHARIOT. Triumph, mastery, superiority, Solar martian influence.**

Legitimate success, merited promotion, talent, capability, aptitudes applied, governmental tact, active diplomacy, competent leadership, reconciliation of opposing interests. Progress, mobility, voyages about the world.	Unjustified ambitions, lack of talent, usurpation, illegitimate government, dictatorship, harmful concessions, dangerous opportunism, cares of management, pre-occupations, overwork, feverish activity without rest.

VIII **JUSTICE. Order, regularity, method, equilibrium, placid lunar influence.**

Stability, converatism, organisation, normal functioning. Law, discipline, logic, coordination adaption to the necessities, moderate opinions, practical sense, reason, administration, economy, dutifulness.	Middle class manners, submission to usage, lack of initiative, slavery to the written word, officialdom, red tape. Police activity, 'legal wrangles, law suits, chicanery, exploitation by lawyers.

IX **THE HERMIT. Prudence, reserve, restriction, Saturnian influence.**

Isolation, concentration, silence, profound study, meditation. Austerity, continence, sobriety, discretion. Experienced physician, occultist preserving his secrets in silence.

Timidity, misanthropy, stubborn silence, exaggerated circumspection, lack of sociability, a boorish character. Avarice, poverty, celibacy, chastity. Sinister conspirator.

X **THE WHEEL OF FORTUNE. The ups and downs of fate, instability, lunar Mercurial influences.**

Sagacity, presence of mind, letting no opportunity pass, happy inspiration, practical type of divination, good luck, fortuitous success as in lotteries. Spontaneity, inventive disposition, liveliness, good humour.

Thoughtlessness, speculation, gambling, abandonment to chance, insecurity. Flippancy, improvidence, bohemian character. Unstable situation, sudden changes of fortune, gains and losses. Adventures, risks, minor fortune.

XI **STRENGTH. Virtue, courage, vital power, Jupiter-Mars influence.**

Moral energy, calm bravery. Mind over matter. Intelligence taming brute force. Subjugation of the passions. Industrial success.

Anger, impatience, immoderate fervour, insensibility, cruelty, conflict, war, violent conquest, surgical operation, vehemence, discord, burning or conflagration.

XII THE HANGED MAN. Abnegation, voluntary self-sacrifice, Moon-Venus influence.

Impartiality, forgetfulness of self, devotion, submission to duty, noble dreams, apostleship, philanthropy, giving oneself. Expansive dreams of the future. What is sown for the future.

Broken good resolutions, unrealized projects, well-laid plans that are never carried out. Unkept promises, unrequited love, kindness of which advantage is taken, being a "mug". Impotence to do what is necessary, Losses.

XIII DEATH. Inescapable fatality, necessary end, disenchantment, active Saturnian influence.

Profound study; intellectual penetration, metaphysics; disillusion, strict judgement, the wisdom of regret, detachment, resignation, stoicism.

Death, unprovoked disaster. Discouragement, pessimism, absolute change, cessation in order to recommence in the diametrically opposite direction.

XIV TEMPERANCE. Serenity, coldness, adaptation, Mercury-Moon influence.

Accommodating character, practical philosophy, freedom from care, acceptance of life as it comes, pliability in the face of circumstances, sociability, educability, adaptive transformation.

Indifference, lack of personality, passive plasticity, inconstancy, changeable moods. Tendency to let things slide, slavery to fashion and to prejudice. Results that fail to come up to expectations, uncontrolled flow of events: things take their course.

XV THE   DEVIL. Disorder,   passion,   sexual   desire, conjunction of Mars and Venus.

Sexual attractions, passionate arousal, magical actions, magnetism, fluidic thaumaturgy, occult power, the exercise of mysterious influences. Activity which protects from psychic attack. Protection from black magicians.

Trouble, over-stimulation, concupiscence, lust, entanglements, follies, intrigues, employment of illicit means, bewitchment, fascination by which one is overcome, enslavement by the senses, weakness in the face of disturbing influences, egotism.

XVI THE FALLING TOWER. Explosion, collapse, fall, Moon-Mars influence.

Childbirth, healing crisis, diffidence, fear discouraging rash enterprises. Benefits derived from the mistakes of others. Common sense, caution, wise timidity. Fondness of pious observances, religious materialism.

Disease fault punished, catastrophe caused by imprudence, clandestine pregnancy, scandal, hypocrisy unmasked. Excess, abuse, hoarding, presumption, pride. Chimerical enterprises, false alchemy.

XVII THE STAR Practical idealism, hope, beauty, Sun-Venus influence.

Candour, abandonment to wholesome influences, naturism, confidence in one's destiny. Flowering of life's possibilities, aesthetics, poetic sensibility, presentiments. Goodness, compassion.

Extravagance, immodesty, levity. Lack of spontaneity, unhygienic artificial compulsions. Day dreaming, romanticism, a mind alienated from practical life.

XVIII THE MOON. Imagination, appearances, illusions, active lunar influence.

Objectivity, the physical world, experimentation, work, hard-won truth. Learning from suffering, imposed task, tedious but necessary toil. Passive clairvoyance, second sight. Navigation.

Errors of the senses, false assumptions, traps, ambushes, deceptions, specious theories, imagined knowledge, idle visions, flatteries, menaces, blackmail, aberrations, travel, fads, lunacy.

XIX THE SUN. Light, reason, concord, solar influence.

Clear discernment, clarity of judgement and expression, literary or artistic talent. Pacification, harmony, good understanding, wedded bliss. Brotherly love, the rule of intelligence and good sentiments. Reputation, glory, fame.

Show, vanity, affectation, histrionics, pride, touchiness. Unappreciated artist. Misery hiding beneath a bright exterior, bluff, empty show, vain pomp, amazing scenery or decor.

XX THE JUDGEMENT. Inspiration, redeeming breath, Moon-Mercury influence.

Enthusiasm, exaltation of spirit, spirituality. Seership, sanctity, theurgy, miraculous medicine. Resurrection of the past, renovation, birth. Propaganda, apostleship.

Spiritual intoxication, mental inebriation, illuminism. Rabble rouser, raiser of spirit forms, Advertising, rumour, uproar, agitation which is nothing but a lot of hot air.

XXI THE WORLD. Achievement,   reward,   apotheosis, Jupiter-Sun influence.

Major stroke of luck, complete success, crowning achievement. Decisive   intervention.   Very favourable circumstances, helpful environment. Absolute integrity. Contemplative   absorption. Ecstacy.

Formidable obstacle, hostile environment, everyone against the individual concerned. Worldliness, thinly spread activities, absent mindedness, lack of application and of concentration. Great reverses, ruin, social disgrace.

XXII THE FOOL. Impulsiveness,   thoughtlessness, derangement, passive lunar influence.

Passivity, absolute abandonment, repose,   renunciation   of   all resistance, freedom from care, innocence,   irresponsibility. Instinctive behaviour, mediumship. Abstention, nothing to do.

Negativity, incapacity to reason or   to   direct   one's   affairs, abandonment to blind impulse, automatism. Unconscious lack of control. Extravagance, Inescapable punishment for stupid actions, vain regret. Self-abasement.

5

CONCLUSION

Games are useful for exercise, and games which exercise the mind develop some precious faculties. It is a good idea to use the twenty-two Arcana (or the trumps) of the Tarot to play at divination. Time will not be lost and, in the course of play, a good deal of serious information will be gleaned by anyone in a studious (Saturnian) frame of mind.

The Tarot can well become the wordless guide of independent Thinkers. It is by handling the pictures, by familiarizing oneself with them in play, that one learns to make them speak. Now, when the symbols take on a significance for us, when indeed symbology in general begins to mean something, we shall be less uncomprehending in the presence of the things which impress themselves on our senses.

By knowing how to decipher the hieroglyphics of life, we shall behave more intelligently and shall cease to be dull creatures who have to learn everything by rote.

We must learn how *to use our imaginations correctly* if we wish to complete our education as reasoners.

Let us use the Tarot wisely.

OSWALD WIRTH
TAROT DECK

*** Based upon original designs by
the Swiss kabbalist, Oswald Wirth
* Authentic colour tones
* The 22 Major Arcana cards include
the 22 letters of the Hebrew
alphabet as depicted by Eliphas
Lévi and popularized by Oswald Wirth**

For the first time the complete 78-card Oswald Wirth tarot deck is available to collectors! Oswald Wirth, a famous Swiss kabbalist, occultist and practitioner of curative magnetism, was a disciple of Stanislas de Guaita, and utilizing symbolical modifications suggested by Eliphas Lévi, Wirth devised a set of tarot cards based upon the Tarot of Marseilles pack. The designs by Oswald Wirth for the 22 Major Arcana cards first appeared in 1889 in a hand-coloured edition limited to one hundred copies. A leaflet supplied with this deck lists the Roman number, Hebrew letter, French title and English title of each Major Arcana card.